بسم الله الرحمن الرحيم

Ref

AMERICAN MUSLIMS:
VOIR DIRE
[Speak the Truth]

Dr. Hislop;

Thank you for being a
member of our family all
these years. I hope
you enjoy this book.

Your Son,

Ahmed Younis

Sep. 21/'02

AMERICAN MUSLIMS:
VOIR DIRE
[Speak the Truth]

Ahmed Younis

MVI
MULTIMEDIA VERA
INTERNATIONAL

Los Angeles, California

ISBN 1-881-50455-7 (Paperback)

Cover Design by Tarik Trad
Images: Copyright © 2002 Photodisc

To order directly from the distributor,
fax request to or write to:
Dawn Books, LLC
556 S. Fair Oaks Ave. #310
Pasadena, CA   91105
(626) 796-3041
dawnbooksllc@juno.com

DEDICATION

The Propet Muhammad said:
Man is on the way of life of his companions,
so watch whom you bring close to you as a friend.

This book is dedicated to the soul and living memory of
Hesham Reda. Hesham's angelic character blessed the
American Muslim community with a passion and beauty found in few people in any arena. He is known
among those who loved and worked with him as
'Mr. Unity.' A rarity in modern day activism, Hesham
exemplified the universal essence of Islam in all his
actions and dealings, regardless of 'the other.'
God willing, young American Muslims will be able to
maintain his unwavering legacy of tolerance
and inclusion.

ACKNOWLEDGEMENTS

I have been blessed with a life full of dynamic personalities and kind hearts, none more dynamic or kind than that of my parents, Dr. Olfat Mohamed and Dr. Samir Younis. I learned critical thinking at home where voicing my opinion was not only encouraged but mandated. You molded a unique and beautiful culture in our home. Your love for God is evident in all that you do for our family and others. I love you.

Thanks to Dr. Aslam Abdullah and MVI for believing in me and publishing this project. Thank you for supporting freedom of speech and information. Without MVI, my voice would have likely been suppressed by those not interested in an honest disscussion of Islam in America.

This writing would not have been possible without the hard work and encouragement of Edina Lekovic. A leader and role model, your talents and personality are indispensable to Islam in America. You are a great friend.

Dr. Maher Hathout honored me by revising the text during its production. Thank you for your humor and friendship. Hathout is an American civil rights leader among a continuity of activists in our nation's history. He has dedicated his life to freedom, equality and self-determination of all people. Today, he stands as a founding father of American Muslim intellectual thought.

Finally, I thank my best friend and compañero Mohamed. With every changing country, culture, language and situation you have been a guiding light. *Venceremos.*

TABLE OF CONTENTS

FOREWORD

Ahmed Younis is a brilliant and passionate American Muslim youth. His upbringing offered him the chance to develop as an individual, comfortable and proud of being himself.

His highly educated parents offered him and his brother the space to develop and grow without inhibition. In the initial years of his life, he was exposed to different cultures and societies, and spent his childhood divided between Egypt, Saudi Arabia and the United States. In California, he attended public schools, then majored in international business at California State Polytechnic University in Pomona , and currently is a law student attending Washington & Lee University in Lexington, Virginia.

His vision to the world was broadened and impacted by the National Model United Nations experience. It is no wonder he is offering us a refreshing look to the future of Islam in America as well as the future vision of America vis a vis Islam.

The main value of *Voir Dire* is in portraying a

vision to the future of Islam in America through the eyes of a person who belongs to this future.

The fresh and refreshing visions are both informative and inspiring. There is youthful carping criticism that reflects love of his country and an enlightened and deep faith in the religion of Islam. It is a very reassuring combination of passion and constructive moderation.

The American Muslim identity clearly emanates in every approach to every topic that the author handles. This is the kind of book that no Muslim youth, or for that matter, any concerned American youth can read without being stimulated to think and without being inspired to act.

I wish the book was more elaborate, to initiate answering some of the questions that it will raise in the minds of the readers and to offer the seeds of suggested projects for action.

Being the first book of a promising young author, we anticipate more to come in the near future.

Maher M. Hathout, M.D.
Senior Advisor of the Muslim Public Affairs Council
Spokesperson and former Chairman of the
Islamic Center of Southern California

PREFACE

In many ways, the American Muslim identity was among the casualties of the terrorist attacks of September 11th. Unlike any other way of life or social movement, Islam was immediately thrust center stage for the stabbing, grabbing, kicking, punching, biting and shooting of those most opportunistic "experts" on the subject. These were the same experts, such as Steve Emerson, who compromised their credibility in the hours after the Oklahoma City bombing in 1995, by misinforming the public about "probable" Arab-terrorist links, that he found through footprint acts of the criminals.

Islam, Muslims and the issues that matter to Muslims all suffered because of the actions of 19 men who acted in disaccord with Islam. As a result, the efforts of organizations that have worked to bring Muslims equality within our pluralism are going to be hindered for a good period. The ears of Americans and their elected officials are being bombarded by a relatively new love affair between right wing fundamentalists and corporate media elites. This must be balanced with the perspective of those who are not profiting off of hysteria.

Before the attacks, the dialogue on Islam within America was crippled by a lack of one important element, an unbiased ear to authentic American Muslim representation. In the mid-1990s, activists complained that when the American Muslim point of view was sought by the media and policymakers, it was to answer questions about the religion of Islam, overlooking the fact that Muslims are Americans too and have input in all facets of our pluralism. Since September 11th, we have regressed from that status to being accused of misinforming Americans about Islam. Daniel Pipes, director of the Middle East Forum, has been among the leaders of the pack in the rush to redefine Islamic concepts (that he has learned through the study of translations of Arabic texts) to suit his spin on issues. In a June 2002 taping of "Nightline," Dr. Pipes attacked Dr. Maher Hathout's credibility and his explanation of the term *jihad* (later discussed in detail).

'Speak the truth' (*Voir Dire*) is the prevalent demand upon Muslims in America by their fellow citizens. The mandate to explain the Muslim reality has exponentially increased since September 11th. Many Americans feel that they have been misled by a significant minority within their population. An example of the results of post-tragedy hysteria is the encouragement of Americans to believe that within the 6 million American Muslims around them, there is a sprinkle of those who are lying in wait for a chance to carry out more attacks. This mentality of fear and uneasiness about the near future, while rightly founded, has led to increased stigmatization of Muslims and their way of life.

The current reality of Muslims of all ages throughout our country reminds me of the venire persons of our jury selection process. Through skilled inquiry, the venire person is required to divulge all that they know of a topic and clearly delineate all relationships they have to a party or group. Similarly, the Muslim in America is expected to prove their patriotism.[1]

I have always been an American Muslim who believes in the reality of the American Muslim identity, although it was not the most popular ideology within circles of youth leadership in Muslim communities. Those who were misguided enough to believe that the American Muslim identity was a dead-end on the journey to true Muslim character have been quieted within the channels of social discourse since September 11th. After falsely believing that Islam and the people of the West or their democratic systems are incompatible, they have been awakened by the results of American Muslim activism as is evidenced in decades of struggle

---

[1] Many non-Muslims, particularly those who "look foreign" have also had to display their red, white and blue to evade hate crimes throughout the country.

through organizations such as the Muslim Public Affairs Council, where I found my ideological roots. From a public, open exchange with the FBI to policy talks at the State Department and on Capitol Hill, MPAC has emerged as the backbone of American Muslim leadership in terms of depth in analysis of sensitive issues and effective activism.

The purpose of this writing is to present one of the *many* American Muslim perspectives on where we fit in the mosaic of the United States. This is not intended to be a definitive argument made by Muslims because to claim a totality is unjust to the working minds of Muslims throughout the world and within our country. To claim that Islam presents a homogenous face is to degrade this needed dialogue to the futility of stereotypes. Although I whole-heartedly disagree with Islamic groups that call for such ideas as a caliph as the only way to lead the people to a felicitous Islamic lifestyle in some far away land, I truly believe that Islam requires those voices of our pluralism to be free to express their views.

To understand how a Muslim perceives the surrounding environment, one must look to the culture of Islam being applied and the environment it thrives in. I say "the culture being applied" because Islam is as diverse as any other force intended to create social change that has come in history.

American social dialogue must vigorously pursue the nature of Islam as it has come to life in its varying forms (both ethnically and ideologically). Only in the

United States does the diverse nature of Islam come to such significant fruition. Upon first glance at some institutions such as the Islamic Center of Southern California, one will find nations represented from all over the world. In fact, I have heard as many languages in such institutions as in the Great Hall of the United Nations.

This essay seeks to clarify the role of the American Muslim identity within the international mosaic of cultures that try to follow the Qur'an and the words and deeds of the Prophet Muhammad (peace and blessings of God be upon him). It represents a continuance from the writing of American Muslim greats such as Dr. Hassan Hathout, Dr. Fathi Osman and Dr. Maher Hathout – from the perspective of someone who has lived within the paradigm that their scholarship and work has so clearly laid down. This is how a young American Muslim who has been involved in living this ideology and bringing it to Americans in a wide range of forums across the country perceives where we are as an American Muslim community, and where we are as Americans in relation to the world.

The topics discussed are only a sample of the myriad of issues to which an American Muslim presents unique analysis and insight that cannot be offered by any other segment of our American pluralism.

A CONTINUITY OF STRUGGLE

"... Our problem has to be internationalized. Now the
African nations are speaking out and linking the problem
of racism in Mississippi with the problem of racism in the
Congo, and also the problem of racism of South Vietnam.
It's all racism. And when these people in these different
areas begin to see that the problem is the same problem, and
when the 22 million black Americans see that our problem
is the same as the problem of the people who are being
oppressed in South Vietnam and the Congo and Latin
America, then – the oppressed people of this earth make up
a majority ... then we approach our problem as a majority
that can demand, not as a minority that has to beg."
Malcolm X, 1965

During my study in Cuba, I had the fortune of
staying at the Superior Institute for the Arts, about
twenty minutes outside of Havana Vieja (Old Havana).
A graduate institution for the arts, the university sits
on land that was once an American country club before
the revolution of the Cuban people in 1959. The country club was for whites only. General Batista, leader of

the country at the time, was allowed to play golf there due to his status but could not become a member because of his dark complexion, which indicated African ancestry. Needless to say, all Cubans of his complexion had no chance of membership or entrance on the grounds of the club.

Among the many young people that I met at the university was a 27-year-old construction worker. Five years previous, he was a *balsero* (rafter) attempting to reach Miami to live with his three brothers who worked in restaurants. He was captured by the U.S. Coast Guard, sent back to Cuba, imprisoned, and fined an exorbitant amount. After five years of working in Havana, he had paid off only 15 percent of his fine. He referred to himself as a *Palestino* (Palestinian) because he was a refugee from Santiago de Cuba and came to Havana to work for American dollars he could not make back home. This young man decided to try the desperate water adventure to Miami because he couldn't get any jobs that paid in dollars and was relegated to doing construction.

Upon relaying this story to the Cuban Deputy Ambassador to the United Nations in a luncheon in New York City, he told me that such a phenomenon is a result of the education of the Cuban people. I completely agree. It is the education of a population that allows them a window to draw parallels with the plight of others throughout the world.

The working minds of people throughout the world make connections, such as the Cuban street culture has made with the situation of the Palestinian people. In Cuba, the people have on many occasions come out to the *malecon* (a strip of highway on the coast) to show their support for the Palestinian people through demonstrations led by President Castro in conjunction with a variety of world leaders. My stay coincided with the visit of the grandson of Ayatollah Ruhollah Khomeini, who participated in a demonstration opposing human rights violations by Israel Defense Forces during the first Intifada (which was non-violent in nature).

The perception that the disadvantaged people of the world have a common bond vis-à-vis the super power of the time has not withered when applied to today's situations of conflict. I write this essay with the backdrop of an image of Ernesto 'Che' Guevara shaking hands with General Gamal Abd Al Nasser in Cairo. In Palestinian refugee camps such as Jenin, Muslim and Christian youth fight with guns in defense of their homeland with the backdrop of historic pictures from the Cuban revolution filling the walls of street corners. Under the portraits of Guevara, the revolutionary Argentine physician, sits the quote: "I am not a liberator, liberators do not exist, it is the people who liberate themselves."

The cause of parallel suffering across the boundaries of race and religion originate from similar environments of growth. For example, there is shared perception between Venezuela and Arab oil states of America's corporate threat to the full enjoyment of their resources. The people of Chile in their failed attempt at bringing Agusto Pinochet to justice before an international tribunal for war crimes, sympathize with a failed international attempt at confronting Ariel Sharon with similar charges in such arenas.

These and other desperations for survival have a sealing force in camaraderie among populations sharing common struggles. For a Muslim, this understanding is pursued in adherence to the law of God.

The Qur'an says: *"O Human Kind! We have surely created you from male and female and made you into peoples and organized communities in order that you may know and recognize (cherish) each other."* (49:13)

Sa'dullah Khan, a South African scholar who has joined the leadership of the American Muslim community, titles his commentary on this verse 'Magna Carta of Human Fraternity.' He writes "Here the false notions of racial arrogance, chauvinism, conceit, sexism and arrogance that emanates from tribalism, racism, nationalism and economic advantage are put to the axe."[2]

Dr. Fathi Osman writes of the same verse:

All of humanity in different places and times is equal in terms of human rights and dignity, and they are one before God, whatever their physical and cul-

---

[2] Sa'dullah Khan, *Dimensions of the Qur'an*, page 71 (1999).

tural differences may be. Tribes, nations and races, as well as languages and cultures may represent a convenient categorization for practical or scientific considerations, but they should never conceal the equal human essence and rights of different individuals or groups, or become barriers among them. Peoples of the whole world should know, not just the names of each other's countries on the map, but the whole material and cultural circumstances of various human groups, so that they may be mutually enriched with their positive characteristics and mutually supported against negative ones. This is the real "knowing" and recognition of one another which leads to universal cooperation and solidarity.[3]

This clearly outlines that the concept of a continuity of human experience is laid down in the Qur'an. The Qur'an mandates a Muslim to recognize the diversity that God has offered to humanity as a blessing. It is a form of worship to recognize the diversity of humanity that God has created, and to use that diversity to advance the cause of what should be common denominators, such as global human rights.

"And among his signs (and wonders) is the creation of the heavens and the earth, and the diversity of your languages and colors; surely, in that are signs (and wonders) for those who really have knowledge." (30:22)

---

[3] Fathi Osman, *Concepts of the Qur'an,* page 121 (1997).

It must be clear that this is not a new and improved Islam, nor is it revolutionary in comparison to the writings of scholars throughout the history of Islamic thought. The *tafsir* (Qur'anic commentary) of Dr. Osman is not liberal in relation to what exists in the mainstream of writings of international scholars of Islam. I recall a meeting hosted by the Islamic Society of Orange County featuring Dr. Yousef Al-Qaradawi, Dr. Hassan Hathout and Dr. Maher Hathout. Dr. Qaradawi is an Egyptian scholar respected as one of the most prominent voices of Islamic thought in modern day. During the meeting, Dr. Qaradawi consistently praised the scholarship of the Hathouts as well as Dr. Osman, citing some of their many accomplishments for Islam in the United States. In fact, during Dr. Hassan Hathout's last visit to Egypt, the Sheikh of Al-Azhar University visited him in his home.[4] So with recognition as mainstream from the most prominent of their peers, the Founding Fathers of American Muslim Thought should be regarded as members of the fraternity of scholars that ignite the critical thinking of all Muslims internationally and for coming generations.

I see a division of labor that aids the advancement of our country. While it is the duty of our leaders in Washington to maintain relations with other states, it is

---

[4] Located in Cairo, Al-Azhar is among the most prominent Islamic academic institutions in modern Islamic history.

the duty of Americans to maintain an understanding of 'others' and their varying cultures and ways of life. Without such, our attempt at leading the world to a more prosperous livelihood will fall victim to the social alliances being created amongst the oppressed in solidarity against our government. The only way we can begin to understand how America is perceived among certain groups domestically and internationally is to allow the representation of voices such as the American Muslim one to be heard.

THE NATURE OF
ISLAM

*"American Muslims face three principle tasks (i) to
transmit their religion fully intact to the next generation
(in a society which is largely permissive and consumerist);
(ii) to demonstrate to the American public the spiritual as
well as the democratic potential of Islam, showing that this
religion is relevant for the solution of most if not all, of
contemporary society's woes ... and finally, (iii) to help
rejuvenate and refocus the Islamic world at large,
particularly through unhampered Islamic scholarship that
concentrates on the essentials of our faith."*
Murad Wilfried Hofmann, Istanbul, 1997

Islam is (or should be) central to the life of every
member of its community. To understand the American
Muslim paradigm, one must be oriented about the cor-
nerstone concepts that characterize Islam. This chapter
is not intended to be a complete dialogue on the
Islamic way of life or its law. It is an attempt to unveil
some common threads and concepts through high-
lights of scholarship on a variety of misunderstood

issues. I am compelled to once again make clear; this is not a liberal, leftist, apologetic, selective or compromising view of Islam's nature. It is mainstream, balanced, moderate Islamic thought as evidenced in American Muslim scholarship with full legal validation under *sharia* (Islamic law).

There has been a barrage of literature and media coverage on Islam since September 11th. Many of the deficiencies that resulted were honest mistakes; the rest (and most vocal) were largely the result of malice by special interest groups. This section will attempt to clarify the honest errors that result from a lack of information.

The most common mistake made among commentators on Islam throughout the world (even in the Muslim world) is that Islam is analyzed through the "modern/western" paradigm of religion. The result of such analysis is terminology like 'Islamic Reformation' and borrowed notions of a separate 'Church' and state. These mistakes are usually made due to a lack of knowledge of Arabic, the historical language of the Islamic texts and the language of the Islamic civilization.

At the most foundational level, Islam, a *din* (way of life) is significantly different in structure from Christianity and Judaism. So although "religion" is a component of Islam, it is not equipped to handle the totality of submission to the will of God in accordance with the message sent to Muhammad (peace be upon him).

"*Din* as presented in the Qur'an, is not a matter of ritual and ceremonial. It is concerned with the broad aim of life and the programme of action by which that can be attained. *Din* gives full scope to man's initiative and discretion. It is meant for a free and intelligent person, a person who has the courage to think, judge and act for himself. *Din* offers broad principles which give guidance to man in the adventure of life and which enable him to attain the goal of self-realization and social welfare."[5]

Murad Hofmann, former German ambassador to Algeria and Morocco and German Muslim scholar, points out that the varying schools of thought "were never a symptom of factionalism, but proof of the liveliness and tolerance of the true pluralism in the circles of Islamic thinking, as characterized by strong academic personalities as Abu Hanifah (d. 767), Malik ibn Anas (d. 795), Muhammad b. Idris al Shafi'i (d. 820) and Ahmad b. Hanbal (d. 855) – none of whom ever intended to found a school (of jurisprudential thought)."[6] It is a fact that many of these scholars attended each other's lectures. This diversity of opinion is the essence of Muslim intellectual thought. To understand the nature of Islam, it is important to understand some fundamental pillars of its teachings.

---

[5] G.A. Parwez, *Islam: A Challenge to Religion*, page 77 (1967).
[6] Murad Hoffmann, *Islam: The Alternative*, page 107 (1997).

Sharia

"The Qur'an shapes the Muslim's mind to consider the priorities in its teachings, and to avoid seeing them in a vacuum, or in a one-dimensional way."[7] Contrary to popular opinion, *sharia* is not codified agrarian social law. This lack of understanding plagues Muslim thought just as much as international commentary on Islam. "They (some Muslims) forget that Islamic *sharia* cloaks the very elements of its flexibility; that some of its provisions lend themselves to change according to a change in circumstances, whereas others do not, and that the latter are minimal."[8]

Sharia is three pronged. The primary source is the literal word of God, the Qur'an. It is complimented with the tradition (*sunnah*: words and deeds) of the last of all Prophets, Muhammad (peace be upon him). The third and most dynamic prong is *ijtihad* (the application of legal concepts to human intellect and deduction of laws to deal with new dynamics that are not addressed in the Qur'an and *hadith*). In his work, *Reading The Muslim Mind*, Dr. Hassan Hathout categorizes the goals of sharia into five. Dr. Hathout's writings clearly refer to the classical categorization of the goals done by third century scholars like Al Shatbi and Al Shafi. Collectively, the objective of *sharia* is the

---

[7] Fathi Osman, *Sharia in Contemporary Society*, page 55 (1994).
[8] Hassan Hathout, *Thus Shall I Stand Before God*, page 49 (1999).

preservation and protection of (1) life, (2) mind, (3) religion (4) ownership and possessions and (5) procreation. For our purposes, we are concerned with the first three.

The first prong of *sharia*, preservation of life, is not limited to the human life. Ecological awareness and respect for the environment are also mandated.[9] A basic understanding of Islam brings forth a conviction that God has provided us with two books: the Qur'an and the book of the universe.[10] A person worships God and contemplates his greatness through enjoying the beauty and power of the natural universe. God explains in the Qur'an that in his creation there are patterns that are a mercy to mankind. American Muslim student leaders aptly coined the phrase, "I am a Muslim therefore I am an environmentalist."

"So too in the creation of yourselves and the animals scattered throughout the worlds; in all these are signs for those assured in Faith." (46:3-4)

Signs in the Qur'an are usually termed *'ayat,'* a word which can also be used for 'verse.' It is interesting that the same word is used for verses of God's word and the natural wonders of his creation. The preservation and strength in connection with both the natural world and the word of God are required for a

---

[9] Hassan Hathout, *Reading the Muslim Mind,* page 44.
[10] Hassan Hathout, *Thus Shall I Stand Before God,* page 26 (1999).

Muslim to truly believe. Dr. Osman writes:

> Signs, which point to the Creator and His wonderful
> creation, are all around people if they are keen to
> think and understand. Throughout the mountains,
> plains, deserts, valleys, forests, salt and sweet water
> areas, and the air there are living creatures, which
> form various communities similar to the various
> human communities. Those who close their senses
> from receiving and understanding the signs of
> nature and life in their enormous variety are choos-
> ing to block themselves from the light of reality, and
> are preferring to live in the deep darkness of igno-
> rance and narrow mindedness.[11]

The second goal of *sharia* is aimed at securing the
mind and and its freedom in all forms, including
speech, writings, art, etc. There is no dissonance in the
Muslim paradigm between mind and faith. Censorship
over the mind should be rejected and no human being
can claim authority over another in this respect. Not
only should the mind be protected from censorship,
but also from repression, fear, anxiety and stress. The
controversial novel *Satanic Verses* by Salman Rushdie
offered a test for the tolerance of those who have
power and call themselves Muslim leaders. Imam
Ayatullah Khomeini issued a declaration for the death

---

[11] Fathi Osman, *Concepts of the Qur'an*, page 44 (1997).

of Rushdie because of his depiction of the Prophet Muhammad and Islam. Historian Karen Armstrong writes:

> Coercion in religious matters is forbidden in the Quran and was abhorred by Mulla Sadra, Khomeini's spiritual mentor. When Khomeini issued his *fatwah* ... he contravened Sadra's impassioned defense of freedom of thought. The *fatwah* was declared un-Islamic by the *ulema* (scholars) of Al-Azhar and Saudi Arabia, and was condemned by forty-eight states out of the forty-nine member states of the Islamic Conference the following month.[12]

In the United States, scholars such as Dr. Maher Hathout staunchly argued for the author's Islamic right to speak his mind and to be refuted intellectually not liquidated physically. Such actions by American Muslims are forgotten or ignored when the Muslim voice is relayed to America at large. Freedom of thought and expression are basic human rights under *sharia* because they are required for the pursuit of full submission to the will of God, which is the core meaning of the word Islam.

"Have you seen such a one who takes as his/her god his/her own whims? Could you, then, [O Prophet] be a

---

[12] Karen Armstrong, *Islam*, page 174, 175 (2000).

guardian over such a person? Or think you that most of
them listen or use their minds? They are but like animals;
nay, they are even more erratic in their way." (25:43-44)

"*God commands justice and kindness and caring for*
(one's) relatives; while He forbids all that is shameful and all
that runs counter to reason (or common sense) and trans-
gression." (16:9)

When a human being neglects his/her unique
intellectual and spiritual merits and allows momentary
desires and whims to always control his/her conduct,
then he/she is behaving like an animal. "The human
intellect is crucial in comprehending the general principles and goals of sharia as represented in the Qur'an
and *sunna,* as well as in understanding the existing
social circumstances and needs which bring the neces-
sity of *ijtihad.*"[13]

Ijtihad is the term indicating the utilization of
available evidence (religious, scientific, statistical and
social) to assay the best course to be taken, provided it
does not conflict with the Quran or *sunnah* or with the
goals of the *sharia.*[14] This allowance for "human inge-
nuity" is key to understanding the American (or any)
Muslim paradigm. *Ijtihad* is not within the absolute
jurisdiction of 'scholars' (*ulema*), but lies within the
auspices of and is a right of every Muslim mind. The

---

[13] Fathi Osman, *Sharia in Contemporary Society,* page 46 (1994).
[14] Hassan Hathout, *Reading the Muslim Mind,* page 43.

preservation of the mind is not only an obligation upon every Muslim, but is needed for Islamic jurisprudence to thrive and become pertinent to modern day. The human intellect should be the fulcrum of complete submission to the will of God for a Muslim. The structure of *sharia* clearly accepts the idea of evolving law. American Muslim writer, and recent law school graduate Asma Gull Hasan writes:

> "The balance that American Muslims have struck between American culture and Islam is, in essence, a de facto Reform Islam. But Islam does not have that many rules that come into major conflict with American life. ... So a "Reform Islam" isn't essential to the American Muslim's existence."[15]

I find this analysis to be in disaccord with the constructs of *sharia*. Due to the existence of *ijtihad*, Islam is reforming and forward-looking by nature. To reform a dynamic body of law that is characterized by change is to canonize the time-sensitive product of human thought (*ijtihad*) and equate its jurisprudential value to other sources of *sharia*. Such results cannot exist parallel to the overwhelming authority attributable to the Qur'an and tradition of the Prophet Muhammad.

---

[15] Asma Gull Hasan, *American Muslims: The New Generation*, page 144 (2000).

Hasan is correct that American Muslims have been able to successfully maintain their ideals while flourishing as members of the pluralism. This, however, is not a reform Islam. It is Islam in its most original form. Only the manner and context have changed, as they should. Hasan's writing is an example of the interpretation of Islam through a framework (western understanding of religion) that is not equipped to handle more than "religion." These are not semantics, they are fundamental principles that must be understood for the dialogue between Muslims and their fellow Americans to flourish in an intelligent framework.

Classically, freedom of religion meant the obligation of facilitating worship for Muslims and others. Today the third goal of *sharia*, should mandate the preservation and protection of religion and worship for all people and all faiths (not just monotheistic religions), as a basic human right. That is a common sense extension of the classical definition as applied today.

Let there be no coercion in matters of faith; the right way has become distinct from the [way of] error; hence, whoever rejects the powers of injustice and evil and believes in God has indeed taken hold of the most unfailing support that shall never give way, and God is All-hearing, All-knowing (2:256).[16]

---

[16] Hassan Hathout, *Reading the Muslim Mind*, page 46 (1995).

It is important to note a nuance in the Arabic of this verse. (*La Ikraha Fi-l-Din*: no compulsion in matters of faith) begins with an emphatic 'No' (*La*). Similarly, the phrase "No god but God" (*La Illaha Illa Allah*) begins with strict, direct and clear language on the seriousness of impressing religion upon someone unwillingly. This is an example of the inherent versatility of the Arabic language that lends itself to such emphasis.

> When one secures his/her human freedom and dignity, he/she enjoys full control over the sources of human power and energy, be they physical, intellectual and/or spiritual-psychological-moral, and thus can face the different changes in life's circumstances with balance and harmony. And this for the human being is *"the most unfailing support that shall never give way."*[17]

Muslims have a right and duty to defend themselves if attacked on account of religion. Likewise, if others are attacked for their ways of life, it is an Islamic duty to defend their freedom of religion.

If God had not enabled people to defend themselves against one another, monasteries and churches and synagogues and mosques – in (all of) which God's name is abundantly extolled – would surely have been destroyed. (22:40).

---

[17] Fathi Osman, *Concepts of the Quran*, page 739 (1997).

Jihad

"Militancy is not the essence of jihad. The greater jihad as explained by the Prophet Muhammad (peace be upon him) is first inward seeking: it involves the effort of each Muslim to become a better human being, to struggle to improve him/herself."[18]

Dr. Maher Hathout writes:

> It is not a holy war. This characterization is Crusade-coinage imposed so repeatedly that even some Muslims adopted the same false terminology. This happens despite the fact that the only thing holy in Islam is God ... the word *jihad* has a root verb: *jahada*, which in Arabic means exerting maximum effort or striving. The theological connotation is striving for betterment ... Holy war gives the impression that *jihad* aims to declare war against non-Muslims all over the world in order to impose Islam as a faith or as a political system by force. Such an understanding, or misunderstanding, ignores the Arabic language, the Islamic sources and the historical practice of Muslims. Islam declares that the only legitimate struggle is to defend human rights – including personal freedom and freedom of faith – as a proper form of *jihad*. It (*jihad*) is restricted to cases of aggression and oppression. Should cases of aggression and oppression occur, Muslims must

---

[18] Ahmed Rashid, *The Rise of Militant Islam in Central Asia*, page 2 (2002).

always fight fairly and be inclined towards peace as soon as an opportunity for a cease-fire presents itself.[19]

"And if they incline to peace, incline to it as well. And place your trust in God. Verily, He alone is all hearing, all knowing! And should they seek but to deceive you (by their show of peace), behold, God is enough for you." (8:61)

Physical *jihad* is allowed for Muslims only to repel those who initiate an attack: *"And fight in God's cause against those who are waging war against you, and do not transgress limits, for God loves not transgressors"* (2:190). Peace and justice are always superior to war for those who are conscious of God.[20]

The "Holy War = *Jihad*" phenomenon is only a glimpse of the campaign of disinformation about Islam to come. *Jihad*, like many others, is a concept that originates from the Qur'an (which Muslims consider the word of God). It is not a political or sociological theory that can be tossed and turned by the whims of activists ("scholars"). It is a tool for betterment, the boundaries of which are clearly articulated in the Qur'an, *sunna* and jurisprudence of scholars (including non-Muslims) throughout the history of Islam.

If Steve Emerson, Daniel Pipes and others are inter-

---

[19] Maher Hathout, *Jihad vs. Terrorism*, pages 17, 18, 21, 67 (2002).
[20] *Ibid*, page 67 (2002).

ested in studying the applications of *jihad* in modern times through a look at its history, they are welcome to. They are, however, obliged to give the historical experience of *jihad* its due weight in their overall analysis. Historical applications are not the totality or even the majority of factors that go into the understanding of *jihad*. These are the rules of jurisprudence of the discipline they attempt to analyze. It amazes me that those who are interested in engaging in scholarship about Islam – like Emerson and Pipes – do not find any obligation to recognize the expertise and authority of Muslim thinkers. If they do not recognize the structure of analysis found in the Qur'an, then their opinions are worthless on topics that originate from it. You cannot explain the rules of baseball by demonstrating on a volleyball court without ever having seen a ball of any kind in your life.

Those who are attempting to redefine the term *jihad* will soon attack other concepts and twist other ideas to suit their political goals. It seems that the conservative fundamentalists (led by the Zionist lobby) of America are working full-throttle to maintain the stigma on Islam and its people.

The violence committed against these words has led and will lead to violence against Muslims and indifference to their struggles. Self-definition is a fundamental human right. We deserve that right like other Americans have before us.

Politics and Democracy

When we study the case of Islam, we find that the principle of separating church and state is obviously inapplicable. Whereas in Christianity there is no (specific teaching about) state, in Islam there is no church, which makes it impossible to project one situation on the other. Office should be held upon personal qualification and posts are open to both Muslim and non-Muslim citizens.[21]

As there is no church, there is also no clergy. *Imam, Sheikh, Mullah, Hujat-al-Islam, Ayatullah* etc. is terminology that indicates experience or academic achievement (formally or informally). In turn, there is no "direct line" or "inside track" to God through any human interveners. Under the rubric of *sharia*, there are no supreme leaders with the unfettered discretion to veto the will of the people. This is clearer in the Sunni schools of thought.

According to the Qur'an, the ruler is the person who is entrusted with authority by the people, and thus is responsible before them.[22] Upon the Prophet Muhammad's death, the selection of his successor took

---

[21] Hassan Hathout, *Reading the Muslim Mind*, page 50, 51 (1995).
[22] Fathi Osman, "Islam and Human Rights" (in book, *Rethinking Islam and Modernity*), page 30, This concept comes from the verse (4:59).

place through an open debate, with more than one con-
tender. Dr. Hassan Hathout sums up the significant
rules governing the process of selection of a leader
through the actions of Abu Bakr:

1. The post must be filled by the mandate of the
   people (Abu Bakr sought the opinion of those not
   in attendance to make sure they concurred).
2. The appointment is conditional. The right of the
   people to give the mandate is coupled with the
   right to withdraw.
3. The ruler is the nation's employee.
4. The head of state is no hostage to the elite, the
   nobility or special interest groups. "The weak
   among you is strong with me until I secure what
   is due to him, and the strong amongst you is weak
   with me until I take from him what is due from
   him."[23]

   I do not posit that the experience of Abu Bakr
should be scientifically applied to all situations. The
situation just after the Prophet's death shows the collective Muslim psyche working its wheels in a point in
history. Unfortunately, most states that have been created in the name of Islam since then have missed this
core concept of collective rule.
   "The Qur'an considers *shura* (collective decision

---

[23] Hassan Hathout, *Reading the Muslim Mind*, page 58.

making) one of the main pillars of the Muslim society, thereby recognizing the role of the people in making the policy and/or decision. In fact, in the Qur'an, *shura* is connected with obedience to God, keeping up prayers and spending money for social needs. (See verse 42:38).[24] The concept of *shura* in application will usually resemble a democracy or republic. The United States' form of a democracy is not an eternally applicable model; any form of legitimate representative government is a democratic system. There are plenty of nations throughout the world where elections are held (some of which are legitimate) and a press exists that are not representative of their people for one reason or another. Those are not democracies. There are concrete models of representative government in Islamic history.

Mr. Murad Hoffmann writes:

> Muhammad Asad has shown in his pioneering book, *The Principle of State and Government in Islam* (1961), that the ideal Islamic commonwealth is a State under the rule of law, a parliamentary republic with a constitution, which could correspond to Western constitutions on all essential points (separation of power, bill of rights, party pluralism, protection of minorities), as long as it ensures that the head of State is a Muslim, that Islam is the State religion,

---

[24] Fathi Osman, *Sharia in Contemporary Society*, page 63.

and that the Qur'an is the supreme constitutional norm.[25]

For every era there is a norm; at the time of the Prophet's death, rule through the voice of the majority was a progressive concept. Similarly, with the *ijtihad* of scholars, those basic constructs of government can be adapted to the modern context of successful statehood. It is important to note that statehood is not required for the application of any of these concepts. The culture of Islamic law is applicable to all situations and magnitudes. In a mosque, for example, the concept of 'rule by majority will' should be applied as it would be for a state.

Human Rights

"There are no major differences between the Western and the Islamic perception of the ideal relationship between citizen and State. On the basis of the Qur'an, the following fundamental rights are guaranteed: life, corporal inviolability, liberty, equal treatment/non-discrimination, property, freedom of conscience, marriage, legal hearing, the assumption of innocence, nulla poena sine lege (no punishment without prior threat of punishment), protection from torture and asylum... fourteen hundred years

---

[25] Murad Hoffmann, *Islam: The Alternative*, page 82 (1997).

ago."[26] Most astounding in Qur'anic law are perhaps the detailed regulations for the self-adjudication, and religious freedom of minorities-evidence of the profound tolerance of Islam. [27]

We have honored (conferred dignity on) the children of Adam; provided them with transport on land and sea; given them for sustenance things good and pure; and conferred on them special favors above a great part of our creation." (17:70)

Dr. Maher Hathout titles his commentary on this verse "Human Dignity:"

Human Dignity has a wider concept than human rights, as dignity comprises the enjoyment of rights and the fulfillment of duties side by side. God granted dignity to humankind since our inception. Thus, the appreciation of human dignity is integral to the Muslim's belief system to a degree that cannot be rivaled by philosophical ideas or laws.[28]

Dr. Fathi Osman posits, that human rights are inseparable from faith in one God:

Defending the human rights of any human being is a religious duty for a Muslim, since he/she believes

---

[26] Ibid., page 113.
[27] Ibid., page 114.
[28] Maher Hathout, *Jihad vs. Terrorism*, page 33.

that any oppression is an obstruction of God's will and plan in His creation.[29] Any discrimination against an individual or group about basic rights as members of humanity is a challenge to the faith, since for any human to claim superiority according to origin or power is contradictory to the belief in the One ultimate Supreme Being.[30] The human rights covered by these five areas (the five goals of *sharia*) include the collective rights of groups and peoples as well as the rights of individuals, and political and social rights have their place side by side.[31]

The Prophet Muhammad (peace be upon him) said: "People are like the teeth of a comb. You are all from Adam: and Adam is from dust. There is no superiority of white over black, nor of Arab over non-Arab, except by piety." The messenger of Islam made this statement over 1,400 years ago. I find it ironic when I give talks in Lexington, VA that I am bombarded with questions about human equality and freedom of thought by members of institutions like the Virginia Military Institute and old dog conservatives from my own university. The glory of America has it that I study at a university shaped around the character of General Robert E. Lee, leader of the confederacy. Although I

---

[29] Fathi Osman, *Sharia in Contemporary Society*, page 10.
[30] Ibid., page 11.
[31] Ibid.

have learned to see him in a little better light than I did prior to living in Lexington, I wouldn't mind if they called it Washington & Justice Powell (an alumnus).

If this is the nature of Islam, why is the portrayal of Muslims so negative? I contend that the ignorance of Muslims is the fuel that our enemies in the world need for their fire. Without an understanding of the foundation of Islamic concepts, it is impossible to produce helpful analysis to issues affecting Muslims worldwide which should fall within our mandate of speaking the truth.

WHY DO THEY HATE US?

Human rights are what reason requires and conscience commands. They are us and we are them. Human rights are the rights that any person has as a human being. We are all human beings; we are all deserving of human rights. One cannot be true without the other ... One cannot pick and choose among human rights, ignoring some while insisting on others.
United Nations Secretary General Kofi Annan

Before his sentencing, American terrorist Timothy McVeigh rose and stated, "I wish to use the words of Justice Brandeis dissenting in *Olmestead* to speak for me. He wrote, 'our government is the potent, the omnipresent teacher. For good or ill, it teaches the whole people by its example.'"[32] Justice Brandeis goes

---

[32] Gore Vidal, *Perpetual War for Perpetual Peace,* page 81 (2002).

on to write in his dissent, "Crime is contagious. If the government becomes the law breaker, it breeds contempt for laws; it invites every man to become a law unto himself."

The Oklahoma City bombing was the greatest massacre of Americans by one of their own since 1993, the year the federal government decided to take out the compound of a Seventh-day Adventist cult (the Branch Davidians) near Waco, Texas.[33] The code name for the assault in Waco was SHOW TIME.

> In defiance of the Posse Comitatus Act (a basic bulwark of our fragile liberties that forbids the use of military force against civilians), tanks of the Texas National Guard and the army's Joint Task Force Six attacked the compound with a gas deadly for children and not too healthy for adults.
>
> The six-hour assault ended only when the building was set on fire then bulldozed by Bradley armored vehicles... More than 80 cult members were killed, of whom twenty-seven were children. The April 1993 'show' at Waco proved to be the largest massacre of Americans by their own government since 1890, when a number of Native Americans were slaughtered at Wounded Knee, South Dakota.[34]

---

[33] Ibid., page 84.
[34] Ibid., page 85.

In a series of notes sent from McVeigh to Gore Vidal, he explained the impetus behind his actions in Oklahoma: "Foremost the bombing was a retaliatory strike: a counter-attack for the cumulative raids (and subsequent violence and damage) that federal agents had conducted in the preceding years." "I decided to send a message to a government becoming increasingly hostile. Bombing the Murrah Federal building was morally and strategically equivalent to the U.S. hitting a government building in Serbia, Iraq or other nations."[35]

The Oklahoma City terrorist act was committed by a white, protestant male who questioned the sincerity of his government through experiences such as being a soldier in Iraq. During that period, McVeigh also wrote a friend: "They (Iraqis) are normal like you and me. They (U.S. government) hype you to take these people out. We've got these starving kids and sometimes adults coming up to us begging for food. I can see how the guys in Vietnam were getting killed by children."

In Iraq, 500,000 women and children died of malnutrition during the first eight years of sanctions. On many occasions, Secretary of State Madeline Albright clearly stated that those deaths were not sufficient to demonstrate that the embargo was unsuccessful against the dictatorship and served merely to punish

---

[35] Ibid., page 108, 109.

the Iraqi people. Saddam Hussein is a prime example of why ad-hoc friendships for strategic advantage are not an effective long-term policy choice. After the war with Iran, Hussein unloaded on Kuwait and once again became an enemy of his former partner, the United States. While we didn't give weapons to Hussein to attack the Kurds (as we did with Turkey), we acquiesced to their oppression and gassing during his alliance with our nation.

In the McVeigh experience, there is no holy war, infidels, abodes of war and peace, crusaders, East v. West, Islamic culture and its applicability to modern time – none of those issues arise. There were no pathetic excuses or slogans defaming Islam as the root of terrorism. Just as Oklahoma was a politically motivated military crime by Timothy McVeigh, Sept. 11 was a politically motivated military crime in the mind of Osama bin Laden, who sanctioned the crime in his tape regardless of the merits of the arguments about his actual direct involvement. Bin Laden and McVeigh share common motivations for their actions, a hatred of United States policy as it came to life in specific situations.

According to the *Los Angeles Times*, 58 percent of Americans were willing to surrender some of their liberties in order to stop terrorism in the aftermath of the Oklahoma bombing. That percentage was dwarfed by polls in the aftermath of September 11th. In fact, the greatest percentages of those who would be willing to give up 'constitutional liberties and rights' were minorities. Have we forgotten about slavery or the detention of Japanese Americans so quickly?

Thomas Paine wrote: "He that would make his own liberty secure must guard even his enemy from oppression for if he violates this duty, he establishes a precedent that will reach himself." Thomas Jefferson, James Madison and the rest of our founding fathers turned over in their graves when right wing Christian fundamentalist John Ashcroft pushed the USA PATRI-OT Act. Such laws are designed to clearly lead to the subversion of several Articles of the Bill of Rights that protect the right to due process, fair and speedy trials and protect citizens from illegal searches and seizures. There is no difference between a conservative fundamentalist taking away my civil liberties in America and a conservative fundamentalist taking away the same rights from a young Saudi, Iranian or Afghan. I make this statement knowing full well that Abraham Lincoln (my favorite President) suspended some constitutional liberties during the Civil War. He was wrong too.

It is fair to assume that Ashcroft and the like don't have an anti-Islam agenda. They have an anti-'other' agenda. Louis Freeh, former director of the FBI carried out similar anti-American actions in defense of our land when Dr. Wen Ho Lee was accused of being a communist spy. The federal judge who dismissed the case clearly articulated that our government embarrassed us in her treatment of Dr. Lee, an American, by suspending his rights merely based on suspicion formed with weak evidence and stereotypes.

As it is being carried out, the War on Terror will be as impotent as the supply-side demolition of Latin America called the War on Drugs. Neither plan attacks the fulcrum of either terrorism or drugs. We continue to wage a war on drugs without healing the addictions of Americans at home (who consume a considerable majority of all cocaine made in Latin America). Similarly, a war on terrorism that does not address the realities on the ground that spawn such violent reactions of desperation as terrorism is not going to advance the image of our nation in the world or our understanding of it.

> An act of terrorism, means any activity that [A] involves a violent act or an act dangerous to human life that is a violation of the criminal laws of the United States or any State, or that would be a criminal violation if committed within the jurisdiction of the Unites States or any State; and [B] appears to be intended (i) to intimidate or coerce a civilian population; (ii) to influence the policy of a government by intimidation or coercion; or (iii) to affect the conduct of a government by assassination or kidnapping.[36]

If this is the definition to be applied, then every

---

[36] United States Code Congressional and Administrative News, 98th Congress, Second Session, 1984, Oct. 19, volume 2; par. 3077 98 STAT. 2707 [West Publishing Co., 1984].

American president since George Washington has engaged in terrorism. Terrorism was waged against the Native American Indians, against our Mexican neighbors in Texas by Stephen Austin, and against the Cuban people through illegal economic embargoes, as defined by the United States code.

When we bombed the largest and most needed pharmaceutical plant in Sudan (*Al Shifa*) in response to the bombing of two U.S. embassies in Africa, we engaged in terrorism. When Sudan sought a U.N. inquiry into the reasons for the bombing, the Clinton administration blocked it. Germany's ambassador to Sudan writes, "It is difficult to assess how many people in this poor African country died as a consequence of the destruction of the Al-Shifa factory, but several tens of thousands seems a reasonable guess."[37]

Throughout history, tyrants have risen among the desperate in all regions of the world, promising change for the masses and a better quality of life. Such characters and their followers exploit the trials and tribulations of the oppressed in order to advance their own political agendas. Osama bin Laden and his circles have been among this group of exploiters and usurpers for more than 20 years. It is no secret that our government aided his inauguration into the world of violence and crime. Noam Chomsky writes:

---

[37] Noam Chomsky, *9-11*, page 49 (2001).

> The United States along with its allies assembled a
> huge mercenary army, maybe 100,000 or more, and
> they drew from the most militant sectors they could
> find, which happened to be radical Islamists, what
> are called here Islamic fundamentalists, from all
> over, most of them not from Afghanistan.[38]

> The CIA did have a role, a major one in fact, but that
> was in the 1980's, when it joined Pakistani intelli-
> gence and others (Saudi Arabia, Britain etc.) in
> recruiting, training, and arming the most extreme
> Islamic fundamentalists it could find to fight a "holy
> war" against the Russian invaders of Afghanistan.[39]

Such mistakes have been duplicated by states like
Israel in aiding and partially funding the creation of
Hamas to counter the Palestinian Liberation
Organization (PLO). Bin Laden and company claim to
be driven by three main concerns on behalf of the
Muslim people: (a) the continuing presence of the U.S.
military in Saudi Arabia, (b) sanctions on Iraq that
have killed hundreds of thousands of children through
malnutrition, and (c) the oppressive, racist policies of
the state of Israel. The State Department offers the
mantra that the Israeli-Palestinian situation is no more

---

[38] Noam Chomsky, *9-11*, page 82.
[39] Noam Chomsky, *9-11*, page 18.

influential as a source of rage than the rest of the griev-
ances on bin Laden's list. If you agree with this analysis, then you lack an understanding of the common culture of resistance that has spread among the people of
the Middle East since the apartheid policies of Israel
were put in place. It is through the Israeli experience
that the Arab people have been convinced of imperial-
ist extensions that continue in their lands until today.
The common denominator of causes in the Middle East
is self-determination. The young people of that region
want to control their own destinies and opportunities.

After the attacks, 'scholars' allowed the U.S. connection to the bombings to bleed over to reputation of
the moderate American Muslim community. Many say
that American Muslims were too slow to comment in
reaction to the terrorism of Sept. 11th. On that day, the
Muslim Public Affairs Council director and senior
advisor were scheduled to meet with President Bush.
Within four hours of the attacks, MPAC had solicited
the condemnation of more than 40 American Muslim
organizations.

I am not responding to the accusations in defense
of our actions, because American Muslims are not
required to do so. I am responding to clarify the record.
Why weren't white Americans asked to condemn the
terrorist attacks in Oklahoma? How many American
Christian groups or militias launched a condemnation
campaign against the actions of Timothy McVeigh?
This is not a frivolous question. It is a question that
every American must ask, if she/he believes in the Bill

of Rights and an all-inclusive, equal pluralism. It is exclusionary and un-American to require American Muslims to prove their allegiance to our nation. Just as America was attacked as a collective, it must respond as a collective. Muslims in America should be held no more responsible for September 11th than Christians were during the aftermath of the Murrah Federal Building bombing.

I had the pleasure of attending a June 2002 lecture by Steve Emerson at the Museum of Radio & Television in Beverly Hills, in which he attacked the Muslim Public Affairs Council for its support of the Holy Land Foundation and claimed the Council has knowledge that Holy Land is a front for financing terrorist activities. Although he gave me a dirty look walking in, I found most of Emerson's presentation to be very informative. He was successful at discrediting some 'leaders' who call themselves moderate Muslims through their own words delivered in public forums.

There were, however, some accusations that I know from personal information were unfounded in truth, of them the Holy Land accusation. Let me highlight Section Three of MPAC's position paper on U.S. Counterterrorism Policy which begins with recommendations for American Muslim organizations. The first of them is:

> All fundraising organizations for foreign, humanitarian causes should have greater financial transparency and institutional accountability. Muslim

organizations should adopt open budgetary policies in which members may inspect the accounting of the organization. Muslims, like most Americans, tend to be very trusting when they see pictures of sick or poor children. Most organizations are legitimate, but it only takes one or two to damage the reputation of others. As a control mechanism, the community has to give responsibly and not be afraid to ask questions.[40]

The Muslim Public Affairs Council is the oldest (and one of few) American Muslim organizations that does not accept a dime from foreign governments or organizations. All fundraising is done within the United States and all money is spent on domestic projects. That can't be said for many domestic organizations that fund the illegal building of Israeli settlements and the militarization of their extremist inhabitants.

One of the main sources of international cognitive dissonance is the politics attached to and the suffering reaped from current Muslim situations. An American Muslim thinks of ethnic cleansing in Bosnia and wonders why world opinion is not reflected in our country. It is very common to hear a young Muslim comment, "They don't condemn Muslim genocide as fiercely as

---

[40] *U.S. Counterterrorism: A Position Paper on Policy*, Muslim Public Affairs Council, page 64 (1999).

they condemn the Holocaust because Americans believe that a Muslim life is not as valuable as a non-Muslim one." Muslims feel as though their worth as a people has been degraded below that of fellow humans. This phenomenon of sub-human characterization is not limited to Muslims. Our government is yet to acknowledge the massacre and exodus of a whole people during the Armenian Genocide because of our interests in not offending a cooperative Turkey in the pursuit of Israeli security.

A great deal of frustration comes from the Arab world in response to world opinion. Suddenly the world is paying attention to people who have been oppressed for decades by quasi-Islamic leadership in the form of tyrants, military dictatorships and kingdoms. One cannot find a dictatorship in the Middle East that was not in some way placed there by (or is a reaction to) United States policies. The democratic aspirations of the Arab people (like their international counterparts) are consistently derailed by our domestic and foreign policies. Why is it that 'experts' who ridicule the Middle East for its lack of democracy don't point to the realities that have shaped those societies into the repressive regimes they are?

If the price of having a democracy in Israel is removing the opportunity for other democracies to arise throughout the region, then that price is too high. It is America's blind pro-Israel policy that maintains a military dictatorship in a number of Arab states, and a fundamentalist religious kingdom in Saudi Arabia. The

democratic aspirations of the Arab people are under-
mined by our foreign policy. The Taliban, are a great
example of what grows in the Middle East as a reaction
to United States' mistakes in the region.

To end the terrorism, we must begin to dialogue
with the people of the world through their legitimate-
ly elected leaders. It is critical for the U.S. to gain credibility with the people of the world, in order to empow-
er them to put more pressure on their governments to
provide free and healthy atmospheres for life. We must
show the people of the world that we want for them
what we want for ourselves. Isn't that the Golden
Rule?

I ponder the actions of President Bush as he keeps
praising our friend Pakistan which stands up for the
ideals of America while he condemns Iran as a member
of the 'axis of evil.' Pervez Musharraf's military junta
and the Pakistani people will not then be inclined to
have elections and a parliament of men and women
that represent their will with such an attitude from the
U.S. Let me make it clear that I am not a supporter of
Iran's supreme guardian councils' unfettered discretion to overthrow a vote, but at least there is a vote. If
policy makers in the U.S. don't begin to see Iran as a
growing democracy, the moderates' of whom must be
supported, we will never regain legitimacy in that
country. I suggest the approach to Iran be entered
through a better understanding of President Khatami's
writings and vision for his nation and the Muslim
world. Democracy in the Middle East and throughout

the world must be a primary United States foreign policy. It is in the best interest of our National Security that the people of the world not feel oppressed by our advancement and prosperity.

If the United States wants to support democracies in the Middle East, then we must push for the free flow of information through media such as Al-Jazeera. This is a prime example of how we get slapped with our own principles. We don't believe in freedom of press in the Middle East because they expose our mistakes as opposed to western sources such as CNN. If we support the Middle East in its pursuit for democracy, we must also hail the reform of the Arab League. For example, the new spokesperson of the Arab League is Hanan Ashrawi, a Palestinian professor and official who exemplifies the strength and leadership of women like President Tarja Halonen of Finland, a nation known for its advancement of women. It is imperative that we allow states and peoples to control their own destinies in what they perceive to be the shadows of a hegemonic super power.

Our mistakes in foreign policy are not limited to the Middle East. In Guatemala, our CIA planned and succeeded in the overthrow of the democratically elected government of Arbenz to replace it with that of Colonel Castillo Armas. Our cause for intervention in Guatemala and other Latin American states was to save the profits and assets of the United Fruit Company, of which top officials in our government had personal financial interests. Corporate interests driving foreign policy are not new to the American political elected and appointed leadership. Henry Kissinger lobbied the government for lenient treatment of the Taliban regime for the purpose of minimizing financial effects on American oil companies whom he lobbied officials on behalf of.

In Chile, Agusto Pinochet Ugarte, who many governments want to try for the genocide, torture and kidnapping of thousands of people was assisted to power by the United States. Most Chileans believe he is guilty and want him tried in a Chilean court.

> With the election of a socialist Salvador Allende Gossens, as president in 1970, despite secret funding of his opponents by the CIA, the White House became involved in a covert attempt to destabilize the new government. The White House's so called "Forty Committee" had approved almost $9 million in secret funds, to be dispensed chiefly to Allende's political enemies, between 1970 and 1973. In September 1973, a military coup overthrew the president, and Washington immediately recognized the new government, led by Agusto Pinochet. The coup ended forty-one consecutive years of democratic government in Chile, the longest period of any South American nation.[41]

During the Kissinger era, many ad-hoc relation-

---

[41] John Allphin Moore and Jerry Pubantz, *To Create A New World*, page 191 (1999).

ships were formed and broken, bringing with them the usual devastation of civilian life. A clear example is that of an understanding between Ford, Kissinger and General Suharto of Indonesia that occupying East Timor would not be an issue for the United States. Shortly thereafter, the massacres of East Timor against Christians and Muslims revealed U.S. allowance to act contrary to international law. Our support of the aggressor Indonesian government continued through the atrocities of 1999; "with thousands murdered even before the early September assault that drove 85 percent of the population from their homes and destroyed 70 percent of the country."[42] The Clinton administration maintained that the situation was under the responsibility of the Indonesian government and that Washington could do nothing to encourage an end to the massacres.

Examples of poor (if not criminal) U.S. foreign policy decisions can be provided from all over the world. Congresswoman Cynthia McKinney writes:

> In 1994, after an act of terrorism killed two sitting presidents, the Clinton Administration purposely failed to prevent the genocide of one million Rwandans in order to install favorable regimes in the region. In 1999, Madeline Albright ok'd a Sierra

---

[42] Noam Chomsky, *9-11*, page 87.

Leone peace plan that positioned Foday Sankoh as Chairman of the Commission for the Management of Strategic Resources, a position that placed him answerable only to the President despite the fact that his terrorist organization raped little girls and chopped off their hands as it financed its way to power with illegal diamond sales. Jonas Savimbi helped the U.S. protect the minority rule of racists in South Africa and his organization continues to rampage across southern Africa in Angola, Namibia, parts of Congo-Kinshasa, and Rwanda without restriction, financed by illegal diamond sales. The continued plunder of Africa's rich resources without penalty and sadly with the knowledge and support of powerful people in the U.S., serves as the foundation of the particular terrorism that victimizes Africans.[43]

Our atrocities in Africa included the usurpation of natural resources such as diamonds, by rich individuals or companies, especially religious conservatives and their media organizations. Our attitudes also included an unwillingness to pressure corporations to loosen their hegemony on AIDS cocktails that needed to be sold in a generic form at an affordable rate for states such as South Africa. I am proud to see our country making significant advancement in facilitating an

---

[43] Congresswoman Cynthia McKinney, "Whose War is This Really?" *The Minaret* magazine, page 27 (May 2002).

increase in availability of AIDS medications for the suffering of African masses.

The people of the world do not hate Americans or our way of life. They hate what has resulted in their lives from the policy decisions our government has taken and continues to pursue. As a nation it is important for the maintenance of future peace, that we understand our role in the international community can be used to prevent attacks on our country and violence against innocents worldwide.

What is American is not determined by elected officials or by appointed czars. American principles are determined by the writings of our forefathers and the frameworks of domestic and international law. In order for us to build 'a community on a hill' we must stay true to our ideals and apply them universally. Democracies are not found wherever there are votes, they are found where the government is implementing the will of the people. Any person who has represented the United States in an international arena knows that it is easy to put together a checklist of atrocities committed against others in the vain name of America.

Our country's attitude must change towards the world. The unanswerable cowboy persona that has haunted the oppressed in fear of repercussions to our decisions must go. Let us enter a new phase in our nations' development in which we gather the support of peoples and nations based on the ideals of America. Let us make it clear to the world that we believe in their enjoyment of the liberties that we have in our land. It is American to believe that an American life and the life of anyone else in the world are equal. It is American to understand that all segments of our society are worried about the repercussions of bad policy at home. Dr. Aslam Abdullah, editor in chief of *The Minaret* magazine, opines in the *Los Angeles Times* (July 3, 2002): "I will ask God to protect this country – my country – and its people and secure them from all ills."

It is un-American to support (directly or indirectly) oppression, disenfranchisement, and poverty throughout the world.

PALESTINE:
A SYMBOL

"Any situation in which 'A' objectively exploits 'B' or hinders his and her pursuit of self-affirmation as a responsible person is one of oppression. Such a situation in itself constitutes violence because it interferes with the individual's ontological and historical vocation to be more fully human. With the establishment of a relationship of oppression, violence has already begun. Never in history has violence been initiated by the oppressed. Violence is initiated by those who oppress, who exploit, who fail to recognize others as persons not by those who are oppressed, exploited, and unrecognized. Consciously or unconsciously, the act of rebellion by the oppressed is an act that nearly always is as violent as the initial violence of the oppressor. Whereas the violence of the oppressor prevents the oppressed from being fully human, the response of the latter to this violence is grounded in the desire to pursue the right to be human."
Paulo Friere, Pedagogy of the Oppressed

There is no Islamic gradation in the value of people or their suffering because of their geographical proximity to historical sites or regions. There is no difference between the plight of the Palestinian people and that of Kashmiris, Kurds, Afghans, Bosnians, Nigerians, Philipinos, Americans etc.

The Israeli-Palestinian "conflict" is, primarily, a domestic policy issue for American Muslims as it should be for all Americans. Although there are historical Judeo-Christian-Islamic ties to the land, the main concern of American Muslims is the human suffering of both the Palestinian and Israeli people.

The reason Palestine is a domestic issue for Americans is two fold. The first, U.S. blind support for the actions of Israel, is fully funded by our tax dollars. Secondly, American Muslims bear the brunt of attacks by "lobbyist organizations" that push such policy. This position is no different from dissenting public opinion during the Vietnam War (presumably we don't want our children to die in wars that don't make sense) and opposition to international nuclear proliferation (because of its negative effects on our security and environment). Blind support for Israel is simply bad for American interests throughout the world, especially in the Middle East.

The Roots of Zionism

In a conference in Basel, Switzerland in 1895, Theodore Hertzl (an atheist of a secular Jewish family) revealed the project of establishing an independent Jewish state. Hertzl exploited sentiments inspired by spiritual Zionism, which were tantalizing at that time to the Jewish mind, and which he planned to replace with political Zionism, whose goal was the establishment of a Jewish state in a place where the local population would not be a real obstacle. Palestine was not identified for this project at the time. Hertzl recommended Mozambique or the Congo for the "homeland." Over the course of the next 20 years, options such as Cypress, Argentina and Uganda arose. Hertzl was disappointed with the worldwide Jewish reaction of the notion of a Jewish state as a political reality of their history as victims of persecution. Near the end of the 19th century, a conference of rabbis in Philadelphia issued a statement saying that the Jews' spiritual mission was incompatible with the establishment of a Jewish political entity. To deal with the reality of existing reluctance, Hertzl settled on Palestine as the only place where fundamental religious emotions could be ignited. The banner of religion was duly raised, emotions ran high, and Hertzl achieved this victory. Political Zionist ideology based the exclusive Jewish right to Palestine on inaccurate historical right.

In fact Jews did live in this area at one time in their long history; they lived there during two periods, both of which add up to a few hundred years. History records that when the Jews entered Palestine, they did not find it empty, and when they left Palestine for the Diaspora they did not leave it empty. Before, after and during the Jewish experience in Palestine, there existed Palestinians in those lands, as mentioned in the Torah.[44]

In 1905, a year after his death, the International Jewish Conference adopted the idea of a home for the Jews in Palestine. During this conference, the Zionists publicized a fantasy that has been swallowed by many until recently, that is "a land without a people, for a people without a land." In 1969, Israeli Prime Minister Golda Meir's reply to a reporter's question about Palestinian rights was, "What Palestinians? I don't see them."

Imagine if the leader of the military force that is occupying your farm, apartment and business denied your very existence. In 1897, Arabs (Christians, Muslims and Jews) made up a total of 95 percent of the Palestinian population and owned 99 percent of land. In 1917, the Balfour Declaration stated: "the British government view with favor the establishment in Palestine of a national home for the Jewish people, provided this does not prejudice the civil and religious rights of existing non-Jewish communities in Palestine." In 1922, the Palestinian population was 757,000 (88 percent of whom were Muslim and Christian Arabs). Although the migrations had begun (and continue today), there was still a worldwide Jewish reaction of disagreement to the creation of the

---

[44] Hassan Hathout, *Thus Shall I Stand Before God*, page 201.

state. The 1920 and 1929, anti-Zionist riots in England preceded riots in Chicago by the Jewish community, appalled at the Jewish representation of Menachim Begin, whom they viewed as a terrorist.

Racism

Israel Shahak, asserts that Mussolini set up squadrons of the revisionist Zionist youth movement Betar in black shirts, emulating his own fascist bands. When Begin became chief of Betar, he preferred the brown shirts of the Hitler gangs, a uniform Begin and Betar members wore to all meetings and rallies at which they greeted each other and opened and closed meetings with the fascist salute.

According to historian Arnold Toynbee, by 1931, labor Zionism was creating "an exclusive preserve for the Jews, what in South Africa is called segregation." Rafael Eitan, former commander in chief of the Israeli armed forces, remarked that anyone who accused the whites of South Africa of racism was a liar, that it was the blacks there who wanted to control the white minority, just like the Arabs wanted to control the Israelis. Shahak is a leading authority on the history of Jews and Zionism among many other topics. Edward Said (an American scholar of Arab descent and Columbia professor) writes in the foreword of Shahak's book:

A Holocaust victim and survivor himself, he knows

the meaning of anti-Semitism. Yet unlike most others he does not allow the horrors of the Holocaust to manipulate the truth of what, in the name of the Jewish people, Israel has done to the Palestinians. For him, suffering is not the exclusive possession of one group of victims; it should instead be, but rarely is, the basis for humanizing the victims, making it incumbent on them not to cause suffering of the kind that they suffered.[45]

I agree with those who claim that Israel exists as a democratic state. It's basic external structure seems to be pretty democratic. At least the elections are free. It is important, however, to un-package some modalities intrinsic in the state's law, distinguishing the Israeli model from others including our own. For example, being a Jew makes a difference in many aspects of Israeli life.

When in the early 1980s, a tiny minority of Israeli Jews emerged which opposed this concept, a Constitutional Law (that is, a law overriding provisions of other laws, which cannot be revoked except by a special procedure) was passed in 1985 by an enormous majority of the Knesset. By this law, no party whose programme openly opposes the principle of a Jewish state, or proposes to change it by democratic means, is allowed to participate in the

---

[45] Israel Shahak, *Jewish History, Jewish Religion*, page xi (1997).

election to the Knesset.[46]

According to Israeli law, a person is considered 'Jewish' if her/his mother, grandmother, great-grandmother or great-great-grandmother were Jewesses by religion; or if the person was converted to Judaism in a way satisfactory to the Israeli authorities, and on the condition that the person has not converted from Judaism to another religion.[47]

> The state of Israel officially discriminates in favour of Jews and against non-Jews in many domains of life, of which I regard three as being most important: residency rights, the right to work and the right to equality before the law. Discrimination in residency is based on the fact that about 92 percent of Israel's land is the property of the state and is administered by the Israel Land Authority according to regulations issued by the Jewish National Fund (JNF), an affiliate of the World Zionist Organization.[48]

Evidence of racism towards Palestinians has been clear since the early days of land clearing operations, and continues today by the Israeli government. Palestinian hospitals are being forced to create mass

---

[46] Ibid., page 3.
[47] Ibid., page 4.
[48] Ibid., page 5.

graves in their parking lots because, as usual, the Israeli military has cornered them into pockets of life – a technique lifted from apartheid South Africa. Israel's vocal support for and cooperation with the former Apartheid government is evident in its treatment of non-Jews. Pockets of Palestinian (Christian and Muslim) refugees are surrounded by military by-pass roads that are off limits to them. In the Occupied Territories today, the results are "cantons" of refugees, whose lives are dominated by the whims of the third largest and most sophisticated military in the world for a nation the size of Jersey. A brief look at maps of the territories before the 2002 incursions shows pockets of civilian life (cantons) surrounded by military by-pass roads that allow no traffic. The Palestinian people have no economy, health facilities, clean water, and schools. They gather for life in slums and refugee camps with only one tool to aid in their advancement, frustrations. It is contrary to our values as a nation to support regimes with such oppressive and brutal practices.

Repercussions at Home

Cuban American National Foundation (CANF) founder Jose Mas Canosa, intended that his lobby would be based on the model of the American-Israeli Public Affairs Committee (AIPAC). Canosa revered AIPAC for its success at monopolizing the market of ideas when it came to Israel. Mas Canosa was determined to subvert the government of President Fidel Castro through political affiliations and U.S. government actions.

The Israeli lobby's success and money has restricted our freedom of dialogue here in the United States more than in Israel. The bias is clear in the print and television media. *The New York Times* is significantly more pro-Israeli-conservative than media throughout Israel, particularly sources such as *Ha'aretz*. There is more open dialogue in the Knesset (Israeli parliament) than exists in our House and Senate. To even remotely hint that Israel needs to be dealt with like any other country (according to international law) among our legislators is to quickly lose friends and campaign contributions.

Mas Canosa and his right wing movement eventually grew to control the dialogue on Cuba and shape the foreign policy of the United States through major donations to members of Congress and Senate. Campaign finance reform is the only way to battle such undemocratic activity. It's just rich people getting the policy they want by financing politicians. What could be more un-American? The exorbitant amount of money that goes to Israel (approximately $15 million per day from U.S. tax dollars) must be curbed for redistribution in projects that actually affect American citizens.

According to Edward Said, the greatest achievement of the Israeli lobby was the "Zionization" of U.S. media. When it comes to the portrayal of the Palestinian situation, we Americans have been led to believe continuous fallacious arguments with no right to refute. Anyone who expressly criticizes the state of Israel is quickly termed either an "anti-Semite" (Arabic apparently no longer being considered a Semitic language), a "self-hating Jew" or if you are in the field of history and disagree with the Israeli governments' account of their history, then you are simply a "revisionist." Among those who have been excluded from mainstream discourse for their points of view are Israel Shahak, Rabbi Michael Lerner, Avi Shlaim and Noam Chomsky. This exclusion of information has cost the American taxpayer $92 billion in free aid since 1967 (Israel was created in 1948).

For those who say that we are creating conspiracy theories and spreading propaganda about the Zionist influence in the United States, I offer this personal experience. I once accompanied Dr. Maher Hathout to a lecture at the University of Judaism in Los Angeles, where he was greeted with the screams of extremists in the audience. Every few minutes during his lecture, someone would rise in the audience and scream at Hathout, calling him a "baby killer" and "hater of Jews." Among the handful of audience members who blurted out comments was Irv Rubin of the Jewish Defense League. From the reaction of other Jews at the forum, it was clear that Rubin was a man whose views were not very popular. All hecklers were kicked out that night and there were no problems. Since then, Dr. Hathout continued to teach courses on Islam at the university.

During my first year of law school, I stumbled

upon a case in our criminal law casebook, *People v. Rubin* (1979). The facts of the case revolve around a parade by the Klu Klux Klan through a predominantly Jewish town. Mr. Rubin gave a speech that was (mis)understood as solicitation of murder. At that point, I thought, one could give Mr. Rubin the benefit of the doubt and say that he was speaking in the 'heat of passion' making loaded comments that could be misunderstood. Then I noticed a note by the editors saying that Rubin was questioned early in the investigation of the killing of Alex Odeh (of the Arab American Anti-Discrimination Committee). When Mr. Rubin once came to the Islamic Center of Southern California screaming and shouting at the front door looking to provoke a physical reaction from someone, I remember being told about Odeh. Due to my natural aversion to conspiracies and the like, I was inclined not to believe the brother who told me of Rubin and Odeh. A bit of law later, I know to trust the casebook.

Before I go on with this story, let me say something that is common knowledge among those who I know well. I didn't think Rubin was capable of anything other than talk. I would always joke with others about him showing up at a talk to hurt someone. I took law enforcement's advice; if the threats are general it usually doesn't mean much.

One night, during a grueling torts memo, I received a phone call from Los Angeles. Irv Rubin and others from the Jewish Defense League had been arrested after their plot to bomb several locations, including the office of Congressman Darrell Issa, the office of the Muslim Public Affairs Council and a Los Angeles area mosque, was exposed by an undercover cop. They are terrorists. Anyone who disagrees is functioning on double standards.

This is the staple domestic terrorism plot: people who are funded by organizations in order to attack and intimidate those who engage in dialogue that is contrary to the predominant pro-Zionist ideology. That presents a domestic threat. It affects the safety of Americans in our country. A segment of our American pluralism (Muslims) is being terrorized and national television broadcasts feel no need to report such situations. There is no difference between Irv Rubin and 'shoe bomber' Richard Reed.

Ariel Sharon

Ariel Sharon is the face of state-sponsored terrorism. God willing, one day he will be brought to justice for war crimes carried out over the last 30 years or more. To understand why, it is important to highlight Israeli actions in Southern Lebanon through the words of Avi Shlaim for a glimpse into Sharon, "the bulldozer" (as his countrymen nickname him). After the assassination of Bashir Gemayel (pro-Israeli Phalange Christian leader) on September 14, 1981, most probably by Syrian intelligence, Ariel Sharon's entire policy in Lebanon was shot. The assassination was a needed excuse for military incursion:

Sharon ordered the IDF commanders to allow the

Phalangists to enter the Palestinian refugee camps of Sabra and Shatilla, on the south side of Beirut, in order to "clean out" the terrorists who, he claimed, were lurking there. Inside the camps the revenge-thirsty Christian militiamen perpetuated a terrible massacre, killing hundreds of men, women, and children. Israel estimated the number of dead at seven to eight hundred, while the Palestinian Red Crescent put the number at over two thousand ... Israeli soldiers got wind of the massacre but did nothing to stop it. The sense of shock and revulsion in Israel and the international outcry forced the government to appoint a commission of inquiry under Supreme Court Justice Yitzhak Kahan.[49]

The Kahan Commission presented its report on 7 February 1983. It concluded that Israel bore indirect responsibility for the massacre at Sabra and Shatila, inasmuch as the Phalange entered the refugee camps with the knowledge of the government and with the encouragement of the army. It recommended the removal of the minister of defense (Ariel Sharon) and a number of senior officers from their posts. Sharon immediately announced his rejection of the findings and recommendations of the Kahan Commission. On February 14 the cabinet decided, by a majority of sixteen against Sharon's single vote, to accept the recommendations of the Kahan report.[50]

Once the PLO had been crushed in its stronghold in

---

[49] Avi Shlaim, *The Iron Wall*, page 416 (2000).
[50] Ibid., page 417.

Lebanon, so the argument ran, all effective Palestinian resistance to the imposition of permanent Israeli rule in the West Bank and Gaza would come to an end.[51]

This is why suicide bombings, regardless of their serious moral and ethical considerations, are such a poor military tool in the revolution against Israeli occupation. Every time a suicide bomber hits, Ariel Sharon gains legitimacy in his incursions, most of which have nothing to do with apprehending suspected terrorists. The recent attacks on Palestinian territories, including refugee camps such as Jenin, are the fruition of Sharon's premeditated (for over thirty years) plan of ousting the Palestinians from what is left of their territories. This is the ideology on which he has based his entire military and political career.

Act I, Scene I of Sharon's recent pre-meditated assault on the Palestinian people was his display of force in arriving to Al Haram Al-Sharif with over 1,000 Israeli soldiers. Since that September 2000 day, Palestinians have been sequestered by the Israeli army in no fewer than 220 discontiguous ghettos and subjected to intermittent curfews often lasting for weeks on end. No one, young or old, sick or healthy, dying or pregnant, student or doctor, can move without spend-

[51] Ibid., page 422.

ing hours at barricades manned by rude and often violent Israeli military officers. Since May 2001, Israeli F-16s have regularly bombed and cleared out Palestinian towns and villages, destroying property and killing civilians and security officials. Apache attack helicopters have used their missiles to murder hundreds of democratically elected Palestinian leaders, for alleged terrorist offenses past or future.

Israel has been engaged in illegal military occupation since 1967, the longest such occupation in history and the only one anywhere in the world today. Israel's cruel confinement of 1.3 million people in the Gaza Strip, jammed like sardines, surrounded by barbed wire-fence as well as 2 million in the West Bank, all of whose entrances and exits are controlled by the Israeli Defense Forces, has few parallels in the history of colonialism. The level of this continued violence escalated significantly under the guise of "fighting terrorism" since September 11th.

Jerusalem

According to historian Karen Armstrong (a Catholic nun for a decade of her life), the first entrance of Muslims in Jerusalem was six years after the Prophet Muhammad's (peace be upon him) death in 638 A.D. Upon a bloodless entrance, the elected leader and companion of the Prophet, Umar Ibn Al Khattab, was toured around the holy city by the Greek Orthodox Patriarch.

Upon sight of Jesus' tomb, the Patriarch asked him

to pray before it, but the caliph refused. Instead, he walked to the middle of the street and knelt in prayer. Umar's explanation was that if he had obeyed the wishes of the Patriarch, it might be used as a future reason for misguided Muslims to claim the place as theirs. This would be contrary to *sharia*, since Christians (and others) must be allowed their holy places free for worship and social congregation. Umar then asked to see the Temple Mount (now known as the Western Wall by Jews), which to his surprise was being used as a trash dump for the city at the time. The caliph began removing the waste with his hands to ensure the law of free religion would be universally applied.

Many Jews explained that they were waiting for the Messiah to return, and that the Temple Mount had no value until then. For Caliph Umar's actions, some Jewish scholars of the time hailed the Muslims as the precursors to the Messiah.

For the first time in Jerusalem, Jews became citizens and Umar brought hundreds of Jewish families to establish residence in the holy city. Jerusalem's status as a cherished place for Muslims traces back to the Prophet's time when the people prayed five times a day facing Jerusalem. This way, their backs were to the idols of Mecca and their faces were toward the land of the people of God. Jerusalem must become a free holy land for future generations. Neither the Israeli nor Palestinian people can control it. Their greed will always come first, and the worshippers of all faiths will have limited access to their holy places.

Conclusion

After more than a decade of barren peace discussions, 50 percent of Palestinians are unemployed and 70 percent live in poverty on less than $2 a day. The disparity in outcomes for Israelis and Palestinians reflect a disparity in leverage between the two negotiators. More settlements were built during Ehud Barak's watch as prime minister than that of his predecessor Benjamin Netanyahu. This is significant because Barak represents the moderates of Israeli politics. Every time Arafat was at a peace table with an Israeli leader, including Rabin (who was assassinated by a Jewish terrorist), leaders like Netanyahu and Sharon launched staunch opposition to peace negotiations. Under the guise of "peace," expropriations and house demolitions increased through the Rabin, Peres, Netanyahu and Barak administrations along with the expansion and multiplication of illegal settlements.

Israel, the settler colony that is the product of imperialism gone badly, with its nuclear weapons capability and its consistent actions and policies that exist above international law, must go. The Israel that is a democracy, that respects the human rights of all its inhabitants regardless of color or creed, and does not function as an apartheid state, must come to fruition. That is the way peace will come to a region that has lived in peace more than it has in conflict.

Meanwhile, our government has funded the consistent oppression of a people for over 55 years with no recourse. I pray that our leadership will implement serious campaign finance reform to put an end to the domination of rich special interest lobbyists in Israel policy as well as others. One day, our nation's policies will reflect to the world that we believe they too deserve the liberties we hold so dear.

A MESSAGE TO
MY PEERS

The crisis of the Muslim mind is not a phenomenon that has suddenly come to our *ummah* (global Muslim community). Our crisis is the product of political and social realities that have culminated in a defeat where it matters most – our ability to ponder and reflect. Our patterns of thought and analysis have become reactions to outside sources rather than the product of our proactive initiatives for the application of Islam in our lives today.

The most treasured component of human faculties for a Muslim is the cognitive ability. Islam in America needs consistent, planned, well thought out work that is directed toward a clear objective. That objective should be to make Islam and Muslims an equal and critical force in the American pluralism that offers a unique perspective on issues that affect our country. We, as the next generation of American Muslims, have an obligation to make that objective a reality in our lifetime.

For every Muslim in the world, there is a responsibility to better their surrounding communities. But for the American Muslim, there is a responsibility to better the whole world.

Never before has God offered young people so many resources and so much potential for change. Not just to change the situation of Muslims, but create change for all people regardless of race, religion, political affiliation or other characterizations.

Young Muslims throughout this country are embarking upon projects that address important domestic and international issues from fresh American perspectives. Elev8, a Los Angeles based group of Muslim and non-Muslim youth, work together to plan, organize and deliver presentations on socio-economic issues to young Americans at schools and community centers on the West coast. They also hold symposia on youth leadership and training. In March 2002, Elev8 led and organized the 1,000 Student March to End Homelessness in Los Angeles. In South Central L.A. sits the Umma Free Clinic. The clinic is one of few in the area that offer free health care for all regardless of health insurance. It was founded by American Muslim medical students at surrounding schools and has always been run by young Muslims.

A major mistake that I have seen in those Muslim communities, who include a significant contingent of youth, is a lack of freedom in thought and expression. I can recall being flown to speak to a large group of Muslim youth. I was immediately disappointed by their collective demeanor. Defeat is all I saw. Their

reluctance to speak their mind in front of their parents
had clearly crippled them by the time they became col-
lege-aged. There was no dialogue because they were
not trained to think, speak or write for themselves. As
I continue to travel across the country, it has become
my belief that young American Muslims are in need of
an intellectual revival. They do not have an identity,
let alone an American Muslim identity. That identity
will only come to fruition if there is a revolution in
Islamic thought.

The role of young Americans is not just one of
activism intended to hold our government responsible
for its actions domestically and internationally. We
are also mandated with interacting with our elected
officials to promote a more healthy dialogue and
remind them of ideals they once held before holding
office. We must tell them that we want to join the Kyoto
Protocol, offer basic health care for all people in our
country, to understand the roots of minority packed
prison systems and ensure civil liberties for all. That is
only the beginning.

When I was nineteen, I had the honor of being
invited by Artists For a New South Africa to meet
President Nelson Mandela on behalf of young Muslims
in America. During our conversation, I asked for
advice about creating significant change in the way our
country thinks about issues. I termed it the 'American
Intellectual Revolution.' Mandela's response was two-
fold: a) he was surprised by my question because he
was told that the average young American is compla-

cent and lazy and b) he told me to build a stronger relationship with elected and appointed officials. In my naivete, I received this prescription for change as though this was a man who knew nothing of our domestic scene. Clearly, I was wrong. Mandela was giving me the advice of historical experience.

A brief look at history shows that it is youth who make change through relationships with decision-makers. Young people have a clear vision of right and wrong without the cloudiness of overbearing cultures or politics.

Politically, young people have been instrumental to change in diverse situations. It was young Cubans who led the fight for independence in Angola. Never forget that the liberation of Angola was the straw that broke the camel's back in the liberation of South Africa from apartheid. In Serbia, it was young activists who rallied the people to overthrow Slobodan Milosevic, a mass murderer, in favor of Kostunica, and the placement of a legitimate government. In Egypt, it was young people who rallied the country in revolt against King Faruk and his cronies in power. Islamic history is riddled with stories of influential youth, of them Mus'ab ibn Umayr, a young Ambassador of Muslims in Mecca to their future fellow countrymen (of all faiths) in Medina before the *hijrah* (pilgrimage) of the prophet. This young man was able to pave the way for one of the first historical constitutions of peace signed among a pluralism of people who reside in a specific area, the Medina Constitution.

My greatest worry for my peers, young Muslims, is that they become intimidated from owning Islam as a part of their identity. Islam should become a part of our daily lives, regardless of whether your parents happen to be Muslim or the country they came from is Muslim or even because friends have shown Islam in a positive light. Regardless of whether you converted to Islam or were born Muslim, Islam needs to become the guiding light within us individually and collectively. At an awards dinner for young Muslim graduates in Los Angeles, I asked them to take an oath:

I pledge to have a perpetual fist raised in my heart in fraternity with those throughout the world and within our country that are suffering. For those who are physically, economically and emotionally oppressed I will dedicate my life. Not because it is cool or "revolutionary," but because it is the essence of Islam. Because I am a Muslim, I am unique. Because I am a Muslim, I am needed in America as it crosses this hurdle in her unprecedented history.

AFTERWORD

Voir Dire: An oath usually administered to a
witness, usually before being sworn in chief,
requiring him to speak the truth, or make true
answers in reference to matters inquired of,
to ascertain his competency to give evidence.
Webster's Revised Unabridged Dictionary

American Muslims must take the initiative to
define themselves. The concept of *Voir Dire* is a way to
spread that definition among our fellow country-
men/women. It is the role of every Muslim, as the
vicegerent of God, and as a citizen of this nation, to
speak truth to power for the sake of justice for ourselves and the people of the world.

The challenge of the founding fathers of American
Muslim thought to the Muslim mind is unique.
Reassert the forgotten and misapplied principles of
Islam by looking forward and bringing Islam to a need-
ed high at this moment in history. A similar challenge

exists for the American mind. Reassert the forgotten and misapplied principles of the founding fathers of our great nation while accommodating the changing landscape of our realities.

This book is not an apology, or defense for a way of life. It is my declaration of independence as an American Muslim.